Mom's BEST Job!

A Children's Book for Moms Dealing with 'Mom Guilt'

It is sad when moms have to leave, but moms have a job to do!

Le'Dor Milteer

3G Publishing, Inc.
Loganville, Ga 30052
www.3gpublishinginc.com
Phone: 1-888-442-9637

©2020 Le'Dor Milteer. All rights reserved.

First published by 3G Publishing, Inc. May, 2020.

ISBN: 9781941247655

Printed in the United States of America

No part of this book may be reproduced, stored in a retrieval system, or transmitted by any means without the written permission of the author.

Acknowledgements

I would like to express my love and appreciation to my husband, Von Milteer as well as my children, Christian and Phoenix, for continually supporting me in my many 'never a dull moment' endeavors. Thank you.

Dedication:

This book is dedicated to my greatest inspiration and loving mom, Doreen Phoenix, the first woman entrepreneur that I ever met.

Some moms build skyscrapers!
They are called architects.

Other moms make yummy food!
They are called chefs.

They work in outer space!
They are astronauts.

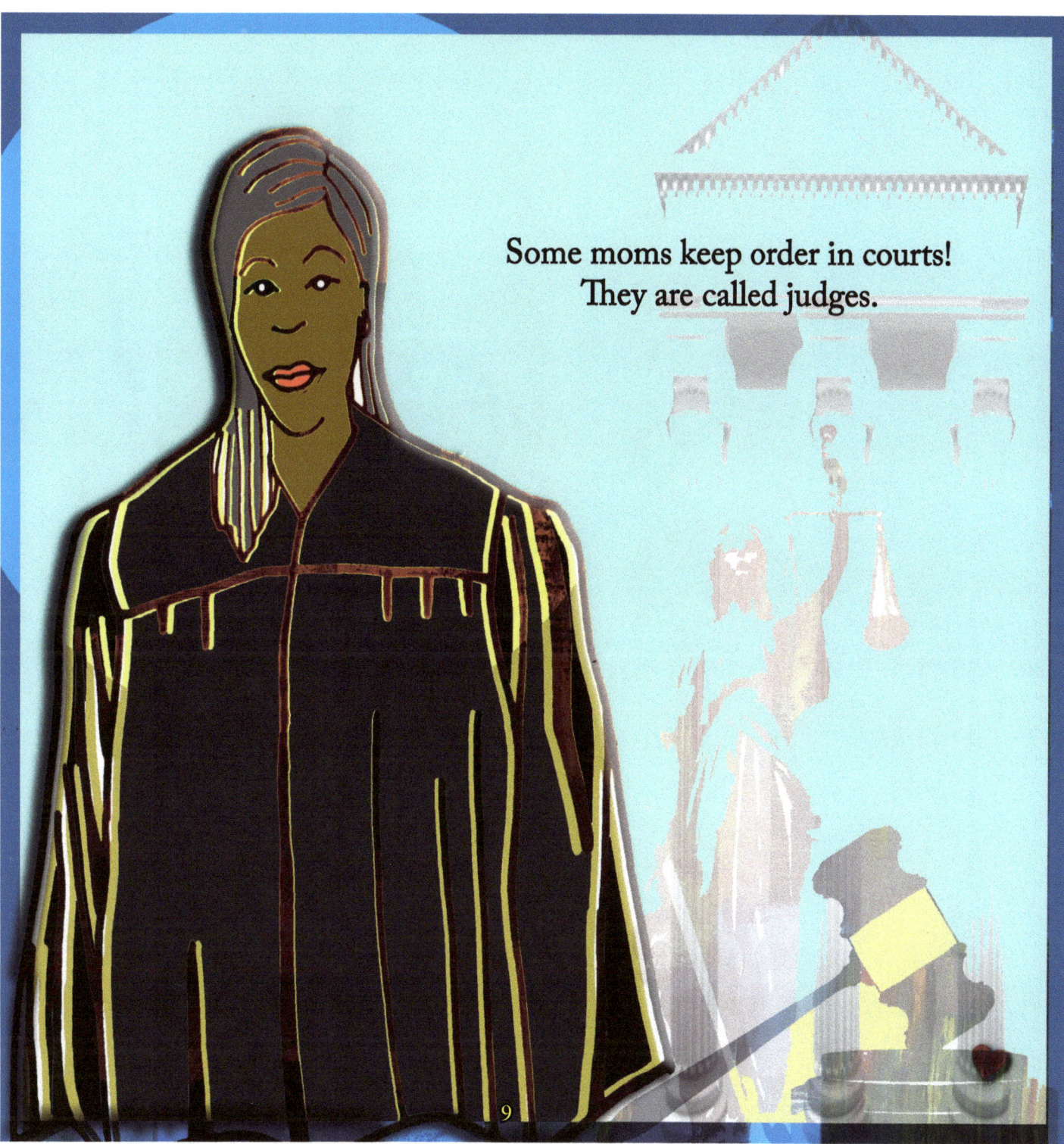

Some moms keep order in courts!
They are called judges.

There are moms who teach!
They are teachers.

Some moms keep your teeth healthy! They are dentists.

They put out fires!
They are firefighters.

Some moms drive trains!
They are train conductors.

14

There are moms who make codes! They are computer programmers.

And there are moms on TV who tell you the news. They are journalist.

Even though moms have important jobs...

MOM'S best job is YOU!

A Poem To Mom:

Mom, I know sometimes you worry
and you are sad when we are a part, but even when you are tired,
you are still pretty and super smart.

Being a mom seems hard but you make it look easy,
working really hard just to please me.
I know you love me and I love you too,
you are my favorite person-
there's something special about you.

So, take extra care of yourself
because I need you around,
here's a tight squeeze for you mom,
you are the BEST mom in town!

www.ingramcontent.com/pod-product-compliance
Lightning Source LLC
Chambersburg PA
CBHW041434040426
42451CB00023B/3500